dabblelab

CREATIVE CRAFTS

SHARE the Love

Projects You'll Love to Give

Mari Bolte

Raintree is an imprint of Capstone Global Library Limited, a company incorporated in England and Wales having its registered office at 264 Banbury Road, Oxford, OX2 7DY – Registered company number: 6695582

www.raintree.co.uk
myorders@raintree.co.uk

Designed by Kayla Rossow
Production by Tori Abraham
Printed and bound in China

ISBN 978 1 4747 4483 6
21 20 19 18 17
10 9 8 7 6 5 4 3 2 1

British Library Cataloguing in Publication Data
A full catalogue record for this book is available from the British Library.

Acknowledgements
All photos by Capstone Studio/Karon Dubke
Background design elements by Shutterstock
Project production by Marcy Morin, Kayla Rossow,
Mari Bolte, Lori Blackwell, and Sarah Schuette

Every effort has been made to contact copyright holders of material reproduced in this book. Any omissions will be rectified in subsequent printings if notice is given to the publisher.

Contents

The passionate crafter can spend hours exploring and reimaging DIYs and how-tos. But what will you do with everything you make and create? Why not share the love? Make someone's day with a piece of art you made just for them. No two projects will come out exactly the same!

Best blocks

A simple piece of scrap wood can be turned into something great! From wall hangings to desk decorations, these bits of wood will brighten anyone's day.

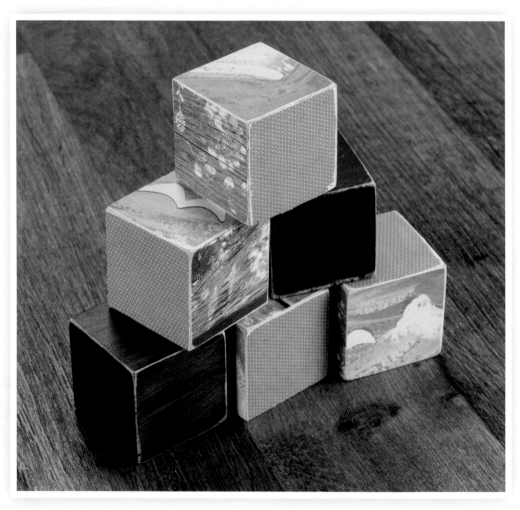

Steps:

1. Cut a piece of decorative paper to fit your block. Paint a thin layer of découpage glue over the block. Gently press the paper onto the block, smoothing out any wrinkles or bubbles.

2. Add more découpage glue over the top of the paper and let dry completely. Then add more glue.

Variations:

• Skip the découpage and just paint the block. Gently rub the edges with sandpaper for a more vintage look.

• Découpage the blocks with pictures instead of paper.

Steps:

1. Paint your chosen piece of wood. Let a little of the natural wood show.

2. Add a thin paint strip in a contrasting colour along the top and the bottom of the wood.

3. Use a pencil to lightly sketch a word. When it's to your liking, fill it in with a dark colour.

4. A light colour along the edges of the word can really make it pop! Add dots, dashes or just solid lines when the word is dry.

5. Use the space beneath the word to show off your art skills! Paint something that means something to you. Hearts, feathers or paw prints are just a few ideas.

Variations:

• If you don't have a steady hand, use stencils to paint on a name or a message.

• Paint several blocks or pieces of wood of various sizes. Choose coordinating colours and patterns. Display them by stacking or hanging them together.

• Give your block a more 3-D look by gluing on wooden letters or shapes instead of painting on words.

7

The greatest greeting

No matter how thrifty you are when it comes to cutting, there always seems to be paper left over. Hang onto favourite designs, prints and textures and make some custom-made cards. Then use them to drop your besties a line!

How to:

Use pieces of scrap paper to create the ultimate mini scrapbook. Cut pieces into squares and rectangles of various sizes and arrange them on the front of a greeting card. Play around with patterns and colour themes until everything is to your liking. Then glue pieces into place.

Variation:

• Trace or sketch a design from a book cover or illustration onto sheet music or a book page. Then cut your design out. Glue it onto a thin piece of cardstock for the ultimate bookmark.

Tip: Photocopy a page from one of your favourite stories.

Variations:

• Cut pieces into geometric shapes, such as triangles or hexagons. Fit pieces together like a custom-made puzzle. Scrapbooking scissors that can cut in scallops, zigzags and other decorative edges can add some extra fun to paper pieces. Or, use an actual puzzle as a template and cut the paper into puzzle pieces instead!

• Use a small round hole punch and cut out a pile of colourful circles. Arrange the circles on the front of a card. You can overlap the pieces or you can space them evenly.

• Don't feel like you have to make a card! Decorate a box, a notebook, a canvas or anything else you can imagine! A layer of découpage glue over the top of the completed project will keep paper corners flat and add some durability.

• Washi tape is another craft supply that always seems to sit around. Use it like you would regular paper. Try layering the washi with the paper. Why not add a weaved design on bookmarks underneath your paper cutouts? Or mix bold strips of tape with smaller accents of paper.

Tip: Leave a pre-printed message! Type a message in a word processing program. Gently attach washi tape to a piece of printer paper. Try to line the tape up with where the text will print on the page. Place the paper in a laser printer and print your document. The ink should adhere to the tape and the tape should easily pull up to be repositioned on your card.

❤ TRY IT!

hello friend

9

Bottled bling

Find your friends at the gym every time when they're carrying around blinged-out beverages!

How to: Use industrial strength glue to cover your bottle with flat back rhinestones. Let the glue dry completely before using.

Steps:

1. Cut a piece of glittery vinyl long enough to wrap around your bottle. It should be wide enough to cover at least the bottom quarter of the bottle.

2. Place a piece of transfer paper over the top of the vinyl. Rub everywhere the paper touches, especially around the edges.

3. Flip the paper over and peel off the back of the vinyl. Carefully position the vinyl over your bottle and press into place. Then rub the paper again. This will transfer the vinyl onto the bottle. Gently pull up the transfer paper.

♥ TRY IT!

Tip: Vinyl placed on rounded surfaces may bubble as it transfers. Use a crochet hook to gently pull up the vinyl to reposition it and get it to lay flat.

Tip: To keep your design fresh as long as possible, hand wash only. A coat or two of brush-on gloss glaze will also help your vinyl last.

Variation:

• Add two or three thin strips of glitter vinyl above the large strip. Leave a small space between each vinyl strip.

Sharp sketches

It's fun to collect permanent markers in every colour. Don't let them dry out before you can enjoy them! Find your friends' favourite colours and doodle something that says, "thinking of you".

How to:

Personalize a plain notebook with permanent marker stars, lines, curves, circles or any other shapes you can imagine. Explore symmetry with mandalas or try your hand at paisley or floral designs. Make it extra special by adding a monogram or a favourite quote.

Steps:

1. Use permanent markers to draw in spots of colour across a plain white cotton pillowcase. Experiment with a variety of shapes and colours - large, plain spots and simple lines are good starts. Then add small dots, swirls, waves or even simple drawings such as feathers or trees.

2. Once your design is to your liking, pour surgical spirit into a spray bottle. Mist over the fabric surface. The alcohol in the surgical spirit will cause the marker ink to run and create a tie-dye effect. Let the alcohol and ink dry completely.

Variations:

• Use black markers (or iron-on vinyl) to write a letter or quote on your pillow. Or use the same technique to create a silhouetted shape, such as an animal or a symbol (like an anchor!)

• Before you start inking, use a hot glue gun to make a design on your fabric. Then follow all the instructions above. Once the alcohol and ink are dry, carefully peel away the hot glue. (If the glue is hard to remove, use a hair dryer on high heat to re-melt the glue a little.)

♥ TRY IT!

Tip: If you have just a pillowcase but no pillow, place a piece of cardboard inside to protect your work surface.

Creative clay club

There's no need to craft alone – why not have a party where everyone can create? Polymer clay is something people of all ages can have fun with. Let guests make their own style of bead or charm. Then let everyone take one of each for a fresh take on friendship bracelets.

Steps:

1. To make basic round beads, pull off a small piece of polymer clay and knead it until it's soft and pliable. Roll it into a ball. Then use a needle to poke a hole through the middle.

2. To add a colourful swirl, roll two pieces of clay into snakes. Twist the snakes together. Then roll the snake into a ball and add your bead hole.

3. With an adult's help, follow baking instructions on your clay package. Keep a close eye on your beads! Once they are baked and cooled, spray them with a polymer clay sealer.

♥ TRY IT!

♥ TRY IT!

Variations:

• Brush on ultrafine glitter before baking. Use a paintbrush to brush off any excess glitter.

• Roll the clay beads in tiny glass beads before baking.

• Gently flatten clay balls into doughnut shapes or ovals before adding a hole. Use a variety of bead shapes on a single necklace.

• With an adult's help, use a craft knife to make random cross-hatch patterns along the main surface of the beads. Once the beads are baked and cooled, gently sand the outsides or sponge with a light layer of acrylic paint. Then seal.

15

♥ TRY IT!

• To make beads for thick metal bracelets, use a knitting needle to poke a large hole in the beads. Press metal eyelets into either side of the hole.

• Roll the outsides of a circle to taper the ends of a round bead.

• For a thick layer of glitter, brush beads with liquid clay and then roll in glitter before baking.

♥ TRY IT!

♥ TRY IT!

Tip: Polymer clay comes in many colours. But you can also colour your own clay by using translucent clays. Mix them with crayon bits, mica powder, powdered pastels or embossing powder.

Charmed by clay

Steps:

1. Press a ball of clay into a flat pendant. Use a straw to cut out a round shape near the centre of the circle. Use a wire to make a hole that goes from one side of the flat circle through the cutout, and then out the other side.

2. Roll the reserved clay you cut out into a bead. Make a hole in the round bead too. Bake both pieces as directed. When you string your beads, string the round bead so that it's centred in the pendant's hole.

Variations:

• Use a regular bead or gem instead of making your own out of reserved clay.

• Make this into an ornament or a key chain instead of a pendant.

• Create a design in the flat clay with stamps and ink.

17

A fine place for flowers

Whether you have a green thumb or just like the idea of plants, flower pots are easy to come by. Fill them with fresh flowers for a May Day or birthday surprise.

1. Give your pots a reverse-drip-dried look! Use acrylic paint to colour your pot, if you want. If your pot has a hole at the bottom, cover it with a piece of tape. Then turn it upside down over a well-protected work surface. Use a drying rack, pieces of wood (such as chopsticks or wood scraps) or upside down cups to keep the edges of the pot off the ground.

2. Squeeze out some acrylic paint out over the centre of the pot's bottom. Repeat with additional colours of paint. Continue adding paint until it drips over the edges of the pot. You can stop now and let the paint trickle down the pot, or you can keep adding paint to cover the entire pot. Whenever you are satisfied with your paint drips, you can stop and let your pot dry.

3. Flip the pot over and sand off any rough edges near the lip of the pot. Seal the pot with acrylic sealer to protect the paint.

Variations:

• With an adult's help, spray paint your pot any colour you like. Use industrial strength glue to attach flat back gems to the pot. Once the glue is dry, coat the entire pot with spray paint again.

• Use balsa wood, tiles, bits of broken pots or sticky back foam instead of gems.

• Skip the paint and glue the gems straight onto the pot. Use a variety of colours.

Tip: For an extra pop, paint the inside of the pot a bold, solid colour.

♥ TRY IT!

Variation:

• Celebrate the Day of the Dead with festive sugar skull pots. Paint your pot white. Then choose where your face will be and paint two large eyes. Add a nose and mouth. Then create symmetrical designs including loops, swirls and dots. Add splashes of colour and use fine-tipped brushes for fine details.

Tip: Sugar skulls are decorated to celebrate a person's life. You can find a lot of design inspiration online. Spend time learning about Mexican heritage - you might learn something new!

Warm fuzzies

Heat up your friends' hands (and hearts!)
by giving them the warm fuzzies.

Variations:

• Use embroidery thread for colour contrast.

• Upcycle an old flannel shirt, sweater or leftover fabric instead of using fleece.

• To use your hand warmers, just heat in the microwave for 30 to 60 seconds. Add a few drops of your favourite essential oil for a nice scent.

Steps:

1. Use a marker to trace or draw a freehand circle onto a piece of brown fleece. Cut it out. Cut out a smaller circle in the centre. Repeat with a second piece so you have a front and a back.

2. Cut a smaller circle out of burgundy fabric. Cut a circle out of the centre. Use scissors to make the outside edges wavy.

3. Stack the burgundy fabric onto a brown circle. Line the centre circles up and sew them together.

4. Pin the two donut pieces together. The burgundy fleece should face in. Sew all three layers of fleece together along the inside circle.

5. Pull the plain brown circle through the centre hole.

6. Sew along the outside edge of the brown circles. Try to stitch as close to the edge as possible.

7. When you have just a small bit of the outside left unsewn, fill with dried oats, flaxseed or uncooked rice – all materials that are safe to warm.

Hot pies

Make hand pies that are (almost) yummy enough to eat. These cheerful warmers are just one way you can put your own spin on a sweet surprise.

1. Use pinking shears to cut circles out of light brown fleece. Cut another round shape with curved edges using white, brown or pink fleece for frosting. Glue or sew the frosting onto one circle. Add long, thin beads for sprinkles. Use more beads or a permanent marker to make faces.

2. Stack the circles on top of each other with the frosting facing up, and stitch together before filling.

Variation:

• Make a fleece bag to store your hand warmers. Measure and cut two pieces of fleece 23 by 46 centimetres (9 by 18 inches). Stack them right sides together and sew down the short edges. Turn the fabric right side out and fold in half with the lining on the outside. Sew up the sides of the bag. Then turn it inside out. Glue or sew hook and loop fasteners inside the bag near the top to keep it closed.

♥ TRY IT!

Yards of yarn

Did you know colour can boost your mood? Logic would say that lots of colour pops could turn a bad day completely around! Use up yards of yarn and make someone smile at the same time with these bright pom-poms.

Tip: To make many pom-poms at the same time, wrap yarn around the back of a chair instead of a fork. Tie loops every inch around the wrapped yarn. Then cut between each loop.

Steps:

1. To make a small pom-pom, gently wrap yarn around the tines of a fork between 90 and 100 times. Cut off the end. Loop a piece of yarn between the centre tines and tie it tightly around the yarn to make a bow shape. Cut off the excess yarn.

2. Slip the yarn off the fork and cut the looped ends with scissors. Use the scissors to trim the yarn into a round pom-pom shape.

Mobile knitting

Hang the perfect present for the yarn lover in your life!
They'll want to display this mobile masterpiece everywhere.

Steps:

1. Cross two knitting needles and use yarn to hold them in place.

2. Make tiny yarn balls by gluing the end of some yarn to a small craft foam ball. Wrap the yarn until the entire ball is covered. Use a small dab of glue to attach the tail end of the yarn. You can make larger balls by using larger foam balls or adding more yarn.

3. To make mini knitting needles, glue a small, round bead to one end of a toothpick. Repeat to make a second needle. Carefully skewer the toothpicks through the yarn ball. Trim the toothpicks to the appropriate size, if necessary.

4. Tie a 15-centimetre (6-in)-long piece of fishing line to a yarn ball. Tie the other end of the line to the knitting needles. Continue hanging yarn balls on the needles, varying the length of fishing line.

Variations:

• Use pom-poms instead of yarn balls.

• Make a garland instead! Tie yarn balls or pom-poms together with a single long piece of fishing line. Leave a little space in between each ball, or push them tightly together. You could also make a necklace. Try alternating pom-poms with beads or smaller poms.

23

Toe-tally custom

Fabric paint is the easiest way to customize clothing. Test out new techniques on socks and give them away as sleepover, sports or spa gifts. Then take it to the next level- replicate your designs on shirts, blankets, towels, pillowcases and anything else that's fit to print.

How to:

Decorate the bottom of your favourite socks with puffy paint. Let the paint dry and you'll have the grippiest, most slip-proof socks ever.

Variation:

• Use a stencil and regular fabric paint on the bottom of your socks. Try something fun, like hoofprints, rainbow stripes or pawprints!

Variations:

• Get more attention with a fully-decorated sock. Draw a V-shape on both the inside and outside of the sock to make a monster mouth. Add teeth and then add any kind of monster you can think of! Sharks, crocodiles, dinosaurs, piranhas and dragons are just a few starting ideas.

• Skip the teeth and go with snakes, frogs, fish or whales instead.

❤ TRY IT!

Sock safari

How to:

Try out basic tie-dye with fabric spray paint. Protect your work surface with newspaper to prevent the paint from soaking through. Turn an empty soft drink can upside down on your workspace. Pull a sock over the can. Scrunch the fabric, varying the size of the folds and the space between each. Then spray the sock with paint. Use plenty for the best colour coverage. Let dry completely before wearing.

Tip: Wash and dry socks before painting them. Follow the instructions on the fabric paint's label for directions on drying and aftercare.

25

An old favourite

Friendship bracelets are a classic gift to give. And because pony beads come in such a wide range of colours, you can customize bracelets for each person. But bracelets are just the start of what you can do with pony beads!

How to:

String two pony beads onto a jump ring. Close the ring. Continue alternating beads and jump rings until the string is as long as necessary. Use a final jump ring to join the pony beads at the ends of the bracelet.

Variation:

• Add small seed beads onto the jump rings for a more feminine look.

Melt a bead

1. You can also melt pony beads! Place a metal cookie cutter on a baking tray lined with baking paper. Set a smaller cookie cutter inside the larger cutter. Pour beads to fill the outline of the large cutter.

2. Have an adult preheat a toaster oven to 205 degrees Celsius (400 degrees Fahrenheit) and bake the beads until they melt. Have an adult remove the baking tray and let the beads cool.

Tip: Go outdoors! Plug in the toaster oven in an outdoor socket, or use an outdoor barbecue grill on high heat. The fumes from the beads can be hazardous in an enclosed area.

Variations:

• Place the small cookie cutter near the edge of the large cookie cutter, instead of in the centre. When the beads have cooled, wrap bracelet wire along the edge of the ornament. Add beads for some interest.

• Instead of the small cookie cutter, place small metal beads around the outside of the large cookie cutter. The metal beads won't melt and you can use the beads' holes for hanging your ornament.

• Sprinkle the hot melted pony beads with small seed beads.

• Make a BFF version by making a smaller charm out of the small cookie cutter. Give away the large piece, with the small cookie cutter's shape cut out, and keep the small cookie cutter charm for yourself.

A brush with creativity

No art room would be complete without pipe cleaners. Bend, roll, twist and wrap projects that you'll actually want to give away as gifts.

Steps:

1. Protect your things by adding some metal armour in disguise. Roll pipe cleaners into flat circles and use glue to keep the ends in place.

2. Trace and cut out a felt circle. The felt should be the same size as the piple cleaner circle. Attach the pipe cleaner to the felt.

3. Continue rolling, cutting and gluing until you have enough circles to cover a tote bag.

4. Start at the bottom of the bag and glue on a row of circles. Overlap the next layer of circles with the first, to create a scale effect. Keep gluing until the whole bag is covered.

• Paint pipe cleaners with sponges. Dab for a subtle effect, or paint the whole pipe cleaner to broaden your colour choices. Add texture and details with permanent markers.

• Twist two pipe cleaners together before rolling them for a swirled effect.

• Use hot glue to attach one end of the twisted pipe cleaners to a glass ornament. Continue wrapping and gluing until the entire ornament is covered.

• Thread beads onto the ends of the pipe cleaner before you start twisting.

♥ TRY IT!

Home sweet home

Sometimes you don't need to visit the craft shop to find amazing art supplies. Tile spacers, landscaping sand and glass blocks are cheap and easy to find in any shop's home improvement section. Or look around your own house – maybe there's something you can use to make a meaningful gift for a friend who's moving away.

How to: Construct something great with tons of tile spacers. They're sold in large bags and are inexpensive – but ask around first. Maybe someone has extras!

Use tile spacers to make a frame for flat plastic picture holders. Line them up for a picket fence look, or overlap them for something more abstract. Industrial strength glue will hold everything together.

Variations:

- Try using spacers everywhere! Use as a backdrop for aquariums or as a border for a mirror.

- Sand is often used for landscaping projects. But it can be used in other ways too! See if you can get your hands on some to make a frame that changes with the tides.

- Stir white glue and sand together until the mixture is runny. Use wooden craft sticks to spread sand along the edges of a frame. Let this layer dry for about an hour. Add another layer, using the stick to create drips and smears. Repeat a third time, if desired. Then let the sand dry completely.

2. Once your design is just how you want it, brush a layer of découpage glue over the glass. Let it dry completely. Then re-colour your design. Add another layer of découpage.

3. Continue colouring and découpaging. The more layers of marker, the deeper the colour will be. When you're done layering, outline your edges with black or metallic permanent marker.

Steps:

1. Try another fixer-upper from the home improvement shop – glass blocks! Clean the glass with surgical spirit before starting. Then use permanent markers to create a masterpiece in the style of stained glass.

Books

Jewellery Crafts (Craft Attack!), Annalees Lim
(Franklin Watts, 2014)

Mother's and Father's Day Crafts (10 Minute Crafts),
Annalees Lim (Wayland, 2017)

Recycling Crafts (Craft Attack!), Annalees Lim
(Franklin Watts, 2014)

Websites

http://blog.hobbycraft.co.uk/craft-ideas/
Packed with tips and tricks to get your creative
juices flowing!

http://www.redtedart.com/
Fun and easy arts and crafts for every season!

http://kidscraftroom.com/
Inspirational art and craft ideas to enjoy
throughout the year.